PATRICIA HUNT

DAVID LIVINGSTONE

Missionary to Africa

D1585865

Hunt & Thorpe

Copyright © 1992 Hunt & Thorpe
Text © 1992 by Patricia Hunt
Originally published by Hunt & Thorpe 1992
ISBN 1 85608 096 X

In Australia this book is published by:
Hunt & Thorpe Australia Pty Ltd.
9 Euston Street, Rydalmere NSW 2116

All rights reserved. Except for brief quotations in
critical articles or reviews, no part of this book may be
reproduced in any manner without prior written permission
from the publishers. Write to: Hunt & Thorpe,
66 High St, Alton, Hants GU34 1ET.

Acknowledgments
Mary Evans Picture Library: cover, title page, 10, 12, 13, 14/15, 17, 29, 36, 41,
    42/43, 44, 45, 48.
The Hulton Picture Company: 6/7, 8, 9, 19, 47.
The Mansell Collection: 20/21, 31.
The Royal Geographic Society: 24/25

A CIP catalogue record for this book is available from the British Library.

Manufactured in UK

CONTENTS

1
NEVER GIVE UP!

Impossible was a word David Livingstone never used. Once he had determined to do something, nothing and nobody could hold him back.

One day when he was about twenty-five, he got up at three o'clock in the morning to walk the twenty-seven miles from Ongar to London and back. He was doing well until, on the way home, he came across a lady who had fallen from her carriage and stopped to help her. He thought of sleeping under a hedge but pressed on instead, got lost, and arrived home long after midnight. He slept soundly for the rest of the night.

A year or two later he began his life's work in Africa, a continent that was largely unknown, except for the coastal areas; its interior was simply a blank space on the map. This did not daunt David Livingstone. He was determined to explore the unknown territory. "I shall open up a path to the interior," he said, "or perish." Although he would die in Central Africa, he did open his path and fill in some of the blank spaces of the map.

Livingstone was a man of immense courage and optimism, one who could never resist a call for help. On one occasion he rode nine miles through forests which were thick with wild animals to help a man wounded by a rhinoceros. This missionary-explorer was a splendid doctor, too.

His African followers thought he had a charmed life and was indestructible, but his real secret was an unshakable faith in God that alone saved him from despair during the constant troubles and misfortunes that he suffered. Despite everything, he could face his friends with a smile, and they said that when he laughed, "he laughed from head to toe." He put his whole attitude toward life into one sentence when he was sent out as a missionary. "Send me anywhere," he wrote, "*provided it be forward.*"

2
STARTING IN A COTTON MILL

David Livingstone was only ten when he started working in a large cotton mill at Blantyre, Lanarkshire, Scotland, in 1825. His work at the mill began at 6:00 A.M. and went on until 8:00 P.M., with only short breaks for the lunch and dinner he brought from home. It was a very hard life for a boy.

David belonged to a very ordinary family that had no money to pay for more education when he left school, but he was determined not to be a mill worker all his life. It was not just that he wanted a more interesting life; he believed that God had important things for him to do. He must educate *himself!* So, with his first week's earnings, he bought the book *Rudiments of Latin*. Clever people could all read Latin, so he had better begin to do the

same! He propped the book on the loom so he could read and learn as he worked.

Even when he left the mill at night his work was not finished, for he went to night school until 10:00 P.M. to learn still more. He loved nature and carefully observed the wild flowers and the birds, as well as collecting flowers and shells, noting down their beauty and design with an accurate eye and careful descriptions in his notebooks. Town and countryside did not provide much entertainment for teenagers in those days, but it would never have occurred to David that there was nothing to do. The whole world was interesting. He was a quiet and thoughtful young man who spent most of his time, when he was not at work, either in the open air or reading at home. Many of his books were about science or other countries. Often his mother would get up at midnight, snatch his books away, and make sure he went to bed. There was little time for sleep, for he had to be up at 5:00 A.M. to go to the mill.

The cotton mill at Blantyre.

3
THE FAMILY

David's parents were good Christians and did their best to make sure that their children grew up to love God. It was a family with high ideals. Truth, purity, and righteousness were important to them, and David was expected to live up to their high standards.

There was a traditional story in the family that when one of their ancestors was dying, he called his children around his bed. "I have searched through all the traditions of our family," he said, "and I never found there was a dishonest man amongst our forebears. If any of *you* take to dishonest ways, it will not be because it runs in your blood! You can only blame yourselves. Take this precept with you: Be honest!"

Neil Livingstone, David's father, was a small tea trader. He was also a deacon at the church, a Sunday school teacher, and a great supporter of missionary work. His wife, Agnes, was a kindhearted

woman, much loved by her children. David's Sunday school teacher, David Hogg, also had a great deal of influence on him. When he was nine, David won a prize for repeating the 176 verses of Psalm 119 with only five mistakes. In his teacher and his parents, David saw clearly what it meant to be a Christian. "Make religion the everyday business of your life," Mr. Hogg told him, "and not a thing of fits and starts."

By the time he was nineteen, David had been promoted to a better job with more pay. Now he had the money to attend lectures at the University in Glasgow, where he studied medicine, theology, and Greek. He had made his great decision: He would become a doctor and give his life to preaching the Gospel.

And he knew where he wanted to go — to China.

(From left to right) the room where Livingstone was born, the house in Blantyre where he grew up, and the home he made with his wife Mary in Ongar.

4
DAVID MEETS DR. MOFFATT

Though David's early life had been restricted and never easy, he never regretted it. He felt that discipline, hard work, and little money had all been good training for the future he planned for himself. A missionary's life would be tough, too!

In September, 1838, he was accepted as a missionary by the London Missionary Society, but he did not plan to go at once. Instead, he stayed in London and enrolled as a student at Charing Cross Hospital to do further training, and finally qualified as a doctor at the age of twenty-seven. Now he would be able to serve the sick and suffering people of China, as well as leading them to Jesus. But he was to be greatly disappointed, for war broke out between England and China, and the door was closed to Chinese missionaries for some time to come.

It was then that he met the great Dr. Robert Moffatt, one of the most famous African missionaries of his time. As they talked, David felt God was pointing him in a new direction. Should he, he asked Moffatt, go to Africa?

The great missionary saw rare qualities in this young man. "Yes," he answered. "We need young men like you in Central Africa. But do not go to an old, established mission station. Push on to the vast district in the north. Up there I have seen, on a clear morning, the smoke of a thousand villages, and no missionary has ever been to them. *That* is where you are needed!"

What a challenge to a young man of David's character. Suddenly he knew where God wanted him to be. On December 6, 1840, he set sail for South Africa and the beginning of his life as a missionary-doctor and explorer extraordinary.

Dr. Robert Moffatt, who became Livingstone's father-in-law.

5
TOWARD THE UNKNOWN

The voyage to South Africa was long and tedious in the uncomfortable sailing ship, and David might well have felt bored and frustrated if he had not been the sort of man who would always find something interesting and useful to do. He made good friends with the captain, who showed him how to use a quadrant, the instrument sailors relied on to find their exact position at sea as they checked with maps and stars. It was a skill that would be very important to David as he explored the vast unknown center of Africa.

It was three months before they reached Cape Town, and from there David began a long, slow, 700-mile journey north by ox-wagon to Kuruman, the mission station established by Dr. Moffatt. It was the farthest mission station from the Cape, but David Livingstone was not to settle there. He was to begin his constant "going forward," and travelled on north to the unknown. In 1842 he settled at Mabotsa, some 200 miles northeast of Kuruman. It was isolated, far from any other white settlers, surrounded by savage and suspicious tribes. Here he began his work of preaching and healing.

Slowly the suspicions gave way to interest. David learned a little of the language the people spoke and did not seem to be the same as the other white settlers some of the people had met. He was caring, instead of rough and bullying. His medicine worked better than the charms of their own witch doctors, and every day someone needed healing. As he cared for them, he talked to them about Jesus, and they listened, fascinated. Soon patients were coming to Mabotsa from as far as a hundred miles or more, not just for medicine.

"Give me medicine for my heart," asked one old man who had listened to Livingstone. "It is proud and angry. Give me medicine to change it!"

6
THE LION

The people of Mabotsa were terrified of the lions that abounded in their territory and often leaped into the cattle pens and tore the cows to pieces. Indeed, there were so many that some people thought their village was under a spell cast by some other village witch doctor. David had no belief in sorcery and spells, only in God. Sustained by his faith and armed only with the spears of the villagers and his own gun, he led a party of them into the bush to drive off the lions.

The Africans would normally form a circle around a lion and try to spear it when it tried to escape, a technique that did not always work. On this occasion it failed badly. One lion was wounded, but all the others broke free. Knowing it was useless to try and persuade the villagers to try again, David set off for home.

Attack from lions was a constant threat.

Then, as they rounded a hill, they found another lion sitting on a rock. David quickly took aim and fired at it.

"He is shot!" shouted the Africans. "He is dead!"

But the lion was only wounded, and very angry indeed. With a roar it sprang at David, grabbed him by the shoulder, and shook him to and fro. David sank to the ground and the lion leaped over him, sinking its teeth into his arm and crunching the bone. Two of the villagers bravely tried to drive it off, but it turned on them, biting them both.

Then, at last, the wounded lion succumbed to its injuries and sank to the ground, dead.

David struggled to his feet and made his way back to the village, but he was never fully able to use his injured arm again.

7

EVER FORWARD

Soon after he returned to Dr. Moffatt's base station at Kuruman, Livingstone married Mary Moffatt, the daughter of the great missionary who had first set him dreaming of Africa. Together they set off for Mabotsa, but not to stay there. Now, they went farther north, to Chonuane, where they established a mission among the Bakuena people. Their chief, Sekhele, an intelligent man, was eager to hear about the Christian God, and then to persuade his people to believe, too. To encourage them, he ordered that they should be beaten until they were converted! He was greatly impressed when he saw David merely telling the people about Jesus and watched the interest in their faces. Some said they believed, even without whipping!

David and Mary lived busy lives, as he explained in a letter. "Building, gardening, cobbling, doctoring, carpentering, gun-

mending, wagon-mending, preaching, schooling...fill up my time. My wife makes candles, soaps and clothes."

But soon they both felt they must move on to other tribes who had not heard about Jesus. In 1847 they set up a new mission about eighty miles farther north, at Kolobeng. Not far away was the immense, dry, hot, empty Kalahari Desert. This was a challenge to David Livingstone, and he began his first real piece of exploration. With hunter William Oswell and Mungo Murray, he set off to find Lake Ngami, of which the African people spoke. It took a long, hard trek of two months before they found it, but they were the first white men ever to see it.

The next year the whole family set off north toward the great Zambezi River. Mary Moffatt was as eager as her husband to carry healing and the Gospel into the unknown, but she and their children suffered so badly from fever that David decided they would have to return to England. His own future, however, lay in Africa. Of that he had no doubt.

. Livingstone was the first white man to reach Lake Ngami.

F A C T S H E E T

D A T E S

March 19, 1813	Born at Blantyre	
1823	Began work in cotton mill	Aged 10
September 1838	Accepted by London Missionary Society as candidate	Aged 25
November 1840	Took medical degree	Aged 27
December 8, 1840	Sailed for Africa	Aged 27
1844	Married Mary Moffatt, in Mabotsa	Aged 31
August 1, 1849	Reached Lake Ngami	Aged 36
April 1, 1852	Wife returned to England	Aged 39
June 8, 1852	Reached Linyante	Aged 39
November 8, 1855	Discovered Victoria Falls	Aged 42
May 20, 1856	Arrived in Quilimane	Aged 43
December 12, 1856	Arrived back in England	Aged 43
February 1858	Appointed H. M. Consul at Quilimane	Aged 45
March 10, 1858	Sailed as commander of Zambezi expedition	Aged 45
May 14, 1858	Reached mouth of Zambezi	Aged 46
1859	Explored River Shire and Lake Nyasa	Aged 46
1861	Further exploration of Lake Nyasa	Aged 48
April 27, 1862	Death of wife at Shapunga	Aged 49
1863	Returned to Zambezi	Aged 50
April 1864	Reached Zanzibar	Aged 51
July 23, 1864	Returned to England	Aged 51
August 1865	Left England	Aged 52
January 20, 1866	Arrived Zanzibar	Aged 52
March 31, 1867	Reached south end of Lake Tanganyika	Aged 54
October 13, 1871	Reached Ujiji	Aged 58
November 10, 1871	Meeting with H. M. Stanley	Aged 58
March 15, 1872	Stanley left	Aged 59
August 15, 1872	Started for Lake Bangweulu	Aged 59
April 29, 1873	Reached Chitambo's village	Aged 60
May 1, 1873	Found dead	Aged 60
April 18, 1874	Laid to rest in Westminster Abbey	

F A C T S H E E T

W R I T I N G S A N D S A Y I N G S O F
L I V I N G S T O N E

"I would not consent to go simply as a geographer, but as a missionary and do geography by the way."

"I have travelled more than most people and with all sorts of followers. The Christians of Kuruman and Kolobeng were out of sight the best I ever had."

"For my own part I intend to go out as a missionary, and hope boldly, but with civility, to state the truth of Christianity.... My object in Africa is not only the elevation of man, but that the country might be so opened that man might see the need of his soul's salvation."

"I am a missionary, heart and soul. God had an only Son, and He was a missionary and a physician. A poor, poor imitation of Him I am, or I wish to be. In this service I hope to live, in it I wish to die."

"If indeed my disclosures should lead to the suppression of the East Coast slave trade, I would esteem that as a far greater feat than the discovery of all the sources [of the Nile] together.

[Writing to the London Missionary Society] "So powerfully convinced I am that it is the will of our Lord I should, *I will go, no matter who opposes*; but from you I expect nothing but encouragement."

"I shall not swerve a hairbreadth from my work while my life is spared."

"I will place no value on anything I have or may possess, except in relation to the Kingdom of Christ."

"My life may be spent as profitably as a pioneer as in any other way."

"I have never felt anyways inclined to turn Churchman or Dissenter either since I came out here. The feelings which we have towards different sects alter out here quite insensibly until one looks upon all godly men as good and true brethren."

"My own order, the honest poor."

[Prayer written in his journal] "Above all, make me useful in promoting Thy cause of peace and goodwill among men."

8
MAN OF MANY PARTS

After he had said farewell to his family in Cape Town and seen them set sail for England, Livingstone returned to Kuruman for the time being.

He was fast becoming an explorer as much as a missionary, pioneering into new or little-known areas. With a great love for Africa and its people, and faced by their sufferings, troubles, and sickness, he was determined to do all he could to make life easier and better for them. As a doctor he spent much of his time healing the sick and treating diseases. At the same time he tried to teach simple laws of hygiene. With few facilities, he had to make do with what was available. The makeshift doctor's surgery and operating theater was a bare table protected by a sheet stretched between two trees. Nearby the people waited quietly for their turn. Medicine or a simple operation followed, and they trusted him completely.

Because there was widespread ignorance as well as poverty, Livingstone had to teach the people to dig wells and make irrigation channels for crops. Reading was irrelevant, for there were no books in their own languages.

Above all, he taught them about the great God who had made them all and revealed himself in Jesus. The simple stories of the Old and New Testaments held their attention and made them eager for more of the truth about the great God. His work as teacher, doctor, and healer led them to regard Livingstone not as a stranger to be feared, as so many white men were, but as a friend.

Why, then, did he concern himself with exploration? Quite simply because he believed that only as the advantages of European culture and the news of the Gospel was brought to them, could their lives be transformed. His exploration was to make new and better routes available into Central Africa.

Livingstone reading the Bible to his men.

18

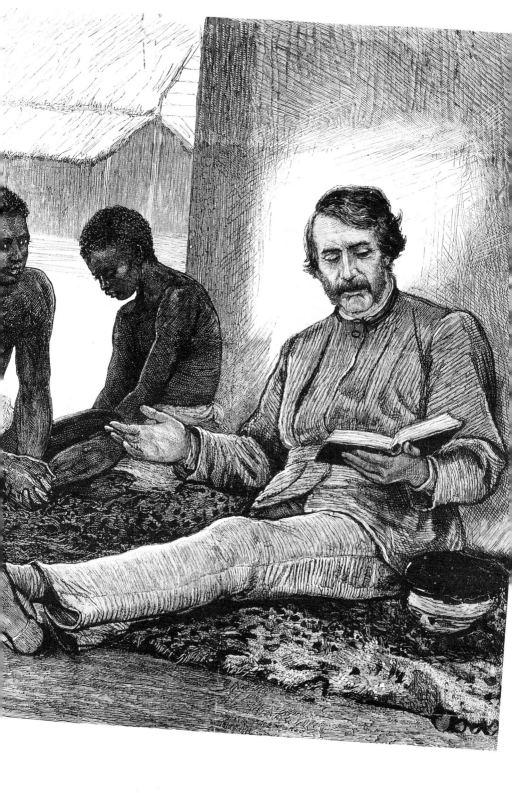

9
WESTWARD TO THE ATLANTIC

After leaving Moffatt's station at Kuruman, David moved on to Linyanti, on the Chobe River. Here the Makololo people lived; their chief, Sekeletu, was already a good friend. But this move was not in order to open yet another mission. Linyante was to be the beginning of Livingstone's most daring feat of exploration, a journey that would hit the headlines of newspapers and scientific journals.

He intended to open up a route from the west coast of Africa to the interior, and he left Linyanti in November 1853 with a party of twenty-seven local tribesmen to plot a way through unmapped territory to the Atlantic coast. He promised his porters that he would see them safely home again, and they trusted his word.

They began by following the course of the Zambezi River

westward, when possible, using canoes made of hollowed-out tree trunks. It was dangerous because hippopotamuses and crocodiles abounded, and canoes could be easily overturned.

Despite the dangers, Livingstone was enthralled by the amazing variety of wildlife — pink flamingos, green parrots, darting blue kingfishers abounded. So did crocodiles, iguanas, and myriads of insects, some of them poisonous. He observed and noted everything in his journals with great care, as a guide to those who might settle there or cultivate the land. But however fascinating the journey, it was always dangerous, with thick bush, unhealthy climate, dangerous tribes, and wild animals. David himself suffered terrible attacks of fever that medicine did little to cure. The party struggled on for month after month, and at times his porters were tempted to desert and try to find their way home, but that would have been impossible without Livingstone to lead the way, and for him there was only one direction to go: forward.

Adventure with a hippopotamus.

10
THE COAST AT LAST

In the middle of the day, when the sun was at its hottest, the party would stop to rest and eat. At night they had to find a place to camp, making shelters from tree branches overlaid with bark and long grasses to keep out the tropical rain. Fires were lit and kept going to keep off the animals that prowled around the camp in the darkness.

Each night before he slept, David would write in his journal, having used his quadrant to plot their exact position. Then he read his Bible and said his prayers for himself, his family, and the African people, whom he thought of as almost his own. For week after week they traveled up the Zambezi, until the river diverged from Livingstone's chosen course. Leaving the river, he led his porters first north and then westward. It seemed that the journey would never end. Then, at long last, they reached the west coast at the port of Loanda.

The toilsome, hazardous journey had taken them six months.

The men from Central Africa were astounded at the expanse of "the great lake" reaching out to the horizon, and at the huge ships in the harbor. They saw them as "big canoes," but some thought they must be floating towns. It took a great deal of persuasion before any of them would venture on board and down below deck.

David was now suffering badly from fever and dysentery, and the captain of one of the ships urged him to return to England at once. But, ill though he was, David Livingstone would not hear of it. He would not leave his task of exploration unfinished. Nor would he desert the men who had served him so loyally. They were now more friends than servants, and he had promised to see them safely back to their homes in Linyante. Leaving the coast at last, he set out to lead them – through the unmapped bush and wild countryside – back to the town they had left six months earlier. It took them *twelve* months to make the journey back.

11

"THE SMOKE WHICH SOUNDS"

Were the eighteen months of perilous foot slogging through tropical Africa, with all the sickness he had suffered, worthwhile? David Livingstone could have no doubt of the answer. Whatever the hazards and the illness, he saw his task as "opening up Central Africa," developing new routes for the people of Europe (especially of Britain), to bring the benefits of civilization to African people without them. Most of all he wanted a route by which more and more missionaries could bring the Gospel. He had shown that the way from the west coast was impractical; now he must try and find a way to the east coast.

In November 1855, Livingstone led a party of Africans on an exploration that began again along the Zambezi River, but went toward the east.

They were to make one astonishing discovery.

From an island in the river they saw what seemed to be smoke rising ahead of them, and heard a sound like terrible, continuing thunder. David described it in his journal. "...a dense white cloud...which had two bright rainbows in it...a great jet of vapour ascending from it, two or three hundred feet high...condensing and coming back in a constant shower which wetted us to the skin."

Below the vapour cloud, hundreds of feet below, was one of the greatest waterfalls in the world, its sound so loud that they could not hear one another speak. Livingstone was the first white man ever to see this marvel, and he named it Victoria Falls, in honour of the Queen of England.

That was in 1855. Years later a town, growing bigger with the years, was built nearby. It was named Livingstone, after the discoverer of the falls.

One of the very first watercolour sketches of the Victoria Falls by the Victorian artist Thomas Baines, who accompanied Livingstone on some of his travels and spent most of his life travelling round Africa, recording the people and countyside. Baines's note on the painting says, "The falls of the Zambezi and singularly redoubling zigzag course of the lower river from a mile and a half or two miles to the SW of the fall. Monday August 11 1862. T Baines." Although Livingstone was the first person to bring the Falls to the attention of the British public, Baines was the first European to picture the spectacle. The local tribespeoples' name for the Falls was "Mosi-oa-tunya," "The smoke that thunders," because of the great continuous roar from the Falls that can be heard from a great distance. Baines's remark on seeing the awesome spectacle was, "How shall words convey ideas which even the pencil of Turner must fail to represent."

25

12

QUILIMANE

Though he was severely ill again with fever, David had no intention of turning back after he found the falls. Instead, he pressed on to a Portuguese settlement at Tete. Exhausted, looking almost like a skeleton, he collapsed. The commandant of the town did all he could to help him recover, including lending him a house of his own. Then fever struck the Portuguese garrison, and David fell ill once more. Not until April of the following year was he fit to travel on.

It was in Tete that Livingstone became acutely aware of the effects of the African slave trade. The town had suffered badly in wars between Portuguese and Africans, but that was not the reason there were too few men to work in the fields or the mines. Many of the villages around about had been ravaged and burned by Arab slave traders, and both men and women were dragged off in gangs to be sold as slaves on the coast.

David Livingstone was to fight against slavery for the rest of his life.

It took another six months to finish his journey of exploration down the Zambezi and along one of its tributaries. Canoes became useless as the river was more and more obstructed by trees, roots, and weeds and made dangerous by river animals. Only in May 1856 did he end his journey at Quilimane, on the coast.

He had accomplished one of the greatest exploratory journeys of all time, crossing the whole of Central Africa from coast to coast. The news of his triumph reached England long before he did. When he arrived there before Christmas in December 1856, he was already famous, though he did not know it. For him it was enough to be back in England for the first time in sixteen years – much of the time without speaking his own language for year after year – and to be with his loved wife, Mary, and the family.

13
A HERO TO THE NATION

When he arrived back in England, Livingstone was greeted by enthusiastic crowds. His return was headlined in newspapers, cheered in Parliament, and Queen Victoria herself sent for him so she might hear at firsthand of his extraordinary travels and discoveries.

Throughout his journeys, David had sent reports of his scientific observations and discoveries, as well as accounts of newly explored territories, to the Royal Geographical Society in London. In May 1855, he addressed the society and was awarded their Gold Medal. His discoveries and reports made it possible to fill in the empty spaces on the map of Central Africa. In 1857 he set down much of his sixteen years' experience in a best-selling book, *Missionary Travels and Researches in South Africa*.

He also traveled throughout Britain, speaking about his work and urging young men to go and help take the light of the Gospel to Africa. His own example was tremendously effective in obtaining volunteers for mission. He was also committed to telling his audiences the horrors of the slave trade and demanding it be ended.

Speaking at the Senate House in Cambridge, he ended with an urgent appeal. "The door to Africa is now open!" he said. "Do not let it be shut again. I go back to Africa to try and make an open path for commerce and Christianity. Do you carry on the work which I have begun!" He spoke similarly at Oxford University, and the following year a new society, "The Universities Mission to Central Africa," was set up. One of its aims was to abolish the slave trade.

David Livingstone himself, however, knowing he was as much an explorer as a missionary, felt it right to leave the London Missionary Society. In 1858 the government appointed him British consul for the East Coast of Africa. It also told him what he was expected to do – mount an exploratory expedition through more of East and Central Africa.

14
THE GREAT LAKE

After eighteen months in Britain, Dr. Livingstone, as he was known, was back in Africa. This time he had several British companions — a doctor, a scientist, and his own brother Charles — though sickness would eventually make them all leave the expedition. Happily, his wife, Mary, was with him, though she was so ill on the sea voyage that he sent her to join her parents, Dr. and Mrs. Moffatt, instead of undertaking the strenuous journey of exploration.

They had brought with them a small steamboat called *Ma-Robert*, though the explorers named it *The Asthmatic* because it wheezed and spluttered so badly! In the end it had to be abandoned as useless, and they continued their explorations from Tete on foot, with a band of some forty carriers from an African tribe Livingstone liked and trusted. David had heard of a "great lake" from the Africans and wanted to put it down accurately on his map. When he *did* discover it, it was one of the most exciting moments of his life. It was immense, beautiful, in lovely country, 300 miles long — and he was the first white man ever to see it.

A little later an Anglican bishop was sent out by the Universities Mission with a group of missionaries to establish a station by the lake, though it eventually had to be withdrawn because of the dangers from hostile tribes.

For David Livingstone, who had toured around Britain denouncing the slave trade in Africa, terrible things were happening by the great lake he named Lake Nyasa, things that almost destroyed all its beauty and wonder.

He was right in the heart of the slave trade, and one of the first things that happened to celebrate his arrival was that he was offered a gift of boys and girls as slaves.

The Ma-Robert on Lake Nyasa.

15
EVIL IN AFRICA

David Livingstone did not stop at refusing to accept the boys and girls offered to him as slaves. He had already made it plain — and he went on doing so not only in his work in Africa but in everything he wrote and sent home — that he was determined to destroy this evil trade.

At the beginning of the century, through the work of the great William Wilberforce, the trade in slaves was ended. Africans were no longer dragged from West Africa to America and the West Indies. In 1832 all slaves on British territories were set free, though it took longer for their freedom to be secured in the United States.

But East Africa was very different. What European nations decided did not matter there. The slave traders were Arabs who had long ago settled on the East Coast. They hunted for slaves through the forests and villages inland, and the Nyasa region was one of their most successful hunting grounds. The things Livingstone and his fellow explorers saw and described in the accounts they sent home were horrifying and almost unbelievable. Time after time they would come across dead bodies by the tracks through the bush, where men and women had collapsed and been left to die. Some were half eaten by wild animals. Others were so badly beaten by the slavers that nothing could be done to help them. Over and over again, they found skeletons and bones, all that was left of women and children.

Everywhere they came across still-smoldering remains of the huts in bush villages that had been set on fire after the slavers picked up all the victims they could cope with and marched their captives — forty or more at a time — toward the big Arab island of Zanzibar.

(Opposite) Slaves were shipped from Africa in brutal conditions. These cross-sections through a slave-trading ship show how they were packed in. Many died on the journey.

16
"SLAVES FOR SALE!"

David did not see the slave market in Zanzibar until he was returning from England to Africa for the third time, some years later. Then he saw a huge space like a cattle market, where slave traders were selling off men, women, and even children to the highest bidder. These terrified people came from all over East and Central Africa. Arabs had lived on this coast for centuries, and the Caliph of Zanzibar was the highest authority in the Arab-African world. He got a profit from every slave sold in the market. They were bought by Arabs living in Africa, exported to Arabia and the Middle East, and sold to the Portuguese settlers, who were often cruel masters.

Over 50,000 slaves were sold in the Zanzibar market every year, and many thousands more in other towns.

On one of his exploring journeys through the bush, David walked into a slaving gang driving their captives on with sticks and whips. When they saw him, the slavers fled, firing their guns uselessly, not daring to risk 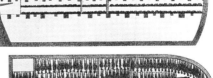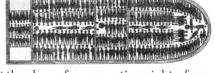 killing a white man. David cut the slaves free, counting eighty-four of them. At other times he did much the same, driving off the traders and freeing their victims, but as he did so, he knew they might well be captured again and that thousands more innocent people would be taken away from their villages while he explored Africa's rivers, lakes, and forests.

There was nothing more he could do but write home and describe the horrors he saw. But one day — *one day*, he vowed — these poor, innocent people should be freed and the slave trade ended.

LIVINGSTONE'S JOURNEYS

David Livingstone's journeys began in 1841 when he first went to Africa, and ended in 1873. During this time he led many expeditions and explored Africa from the Cape to Lake Victoria and from the Atlantic to the Indian Ocean.

His first eight years were spent exploring Southern Africa, building mission stations in Bechuanaland and crossing the Kalahari Desert to Lake Ngami.

Livingstone's first major expedition, in 1850, crossed the continent from Luanda on the Atlantic coast to Quilimane on the Indian Ocean. On his return journey he visited (and named) the newly-discovered Victoria Falls.

His next journey, in 1866, was northward in an effort to discover the source of the Nile. After the meeting with Stanley at Ujiji in 1871 he continued his search, and after prolonged ill health Livingstone died in a village on the shores of Lake Bangweulu, very near to the source of the Nile.

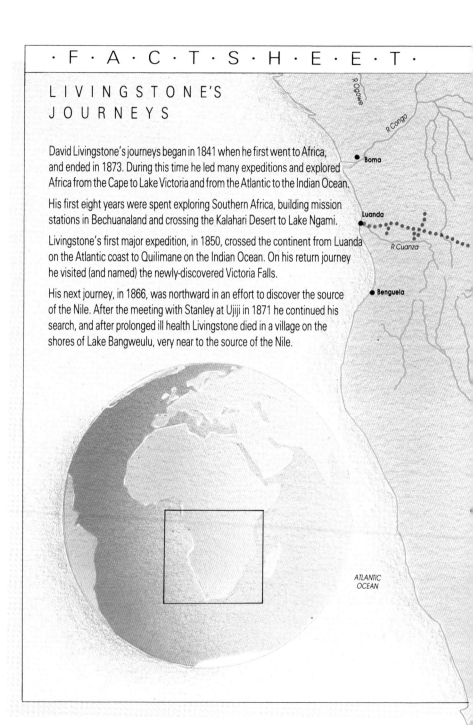

R Ogowe

R Congo

Boma

Luanda

R Cuanza

Benguela

ATLANTIC OCEAN

Cape Town

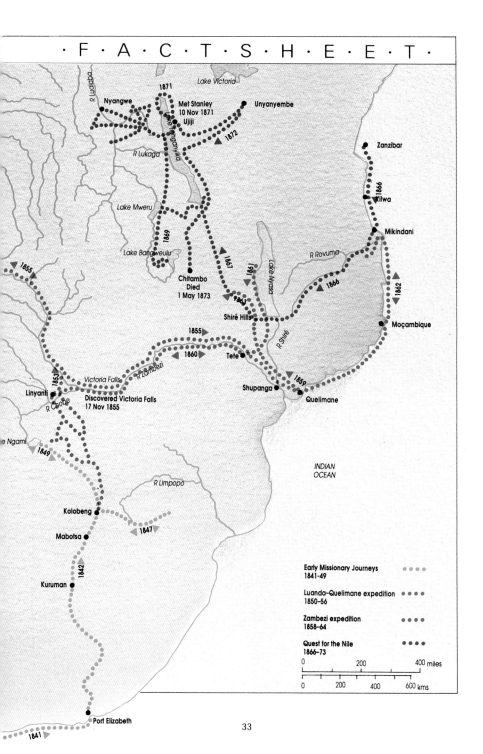

Lake Victoria

1871

Nyangwe

Met Stanley
10 Nov 1871
Ujiji

Unyanyembe

R Lualaba

R Lukaga

Lake Tanganyika

1872

Zanzibar

1866

Kilwa

Lake Mweru

Mikindani

1869

Lake Bangweulu

R Rovuma

1867

1861

Lake Nyasa

1866

1862

Chitambo
Died
1 May 1873

1863

Shiré Hills

Moçambique

1855

1855

1860

Tete

R Shiré

R Zambezi

Victoria Falls

1853

Linyanti

Discovered Victoria Falls
17 Nov 1855

R Chobe

Shupanga

1859

Quelimane

e Ngami

1849

R Limpopo

INDIAN
OCEAN

Kolobeng

1847

Mabotsa

1842

Kuruman

Early Missionary Journeys
1841-49

Luanda–Quelimane expedition
1850–56

Zambezi expedition
1858–64

Quest for the Nile
1866–73

| 0 | 200 | 400 miles |

| 0 | 200 | 400 | 600 kms |

Port Elizabeth

1841

33

17
"THE WORST DAY OF MY LIFE!"

Livingstone's first sixteen years in Africa had been given to exploring across immense distances, trying to find a route across Africa for commerce and the Christian missionaries. This second period was much shorter – only six years – and David spent it mapping the lower reaches of the Zambezi, exploring in the Shiré hills overlooking Lake Nyasa, and traveling the lake itself. He was fortunate to have a new steam boat when the *Ma-Robert* practically came to pieces. This one could be taken apart, carried by porters over falls and rapids, and put together again without difficulty. It would be a great help in his exploration.

It was a difficult, often dangerous, and always lonely life. He missed his family dreadfully, and especially his dear wife, Mary, whom he had left behind at Cape Town. From there she had gone to her parents, the Moffatts, returned to England with a new baby and now, at last, was coming to join her husband. In January 1862, she arrived at Lake Nyasa with the first group of missionaries for the region. David had met them at the coast and brought them home – and it *was* to be "home" for them all. Mary found it all more beautiful and exciting than her husband had described. She traveled with him on the lake, down through the bush paths, and sat in their little house planning all the things he would do in the future, the other great journeys he would make, and whether she would be able to go on them all with him.

Then, three months after she arrived, Mary caught a fever and died.

"It is the worst day of my life," wrote David in his journal.

All the joy had gone out of his adventures, and he did not know what to do.

18
MISSION RECALLED

David had not only lost his wife, whom he buried at Shapunga, where a white cross marked her grave for a century and more. His brother Charles, who was still with him, fell ill with dysentery and had to return to England. More important to the expedition, Dr. Kirk, the naturalist, fell ill and also had to return. Then David, who had always suffered from one or another of the dreadful African fevers, collapsed again. He had lost three of the people most dear to him and had no great wish to go on.

As he continued to explore the Shiré country and the hills, he found constant evidence of the slavers: burned villages, skeletons by the roadside, and famine because there were not enough men to till the ground and care for the crops.

It was no great surprise when he received a letter from the British government recalling the exploratory mission of which he was the head. He did not particularly want to go home to England, but had no heart to stay in Africa. It was the worst period of his life.

Reaching England in July 1864, he again found the crowds cheering "Doctor Livingstone!" wherever he went. But this time he had no enthusiasm for it and spent three months resting and recovering at the home of a friend.

Then, before a year had gone by, he was thinking of Africa again. Would he be willing to go back, asked the head of the Royal Geographical Society, to explore in new regions, to fill in more of the empty spaces on the map?

Now he had no hesitation. Yes, he *would* go; he *wanted* to go back. His heart was in Africa! Just over a year after he had come to England, he set sail again for East Africa. But this time, he would not come back.

SAYINGS ABOUT DAVID LIVINGSTONE

Sir Henry Johnstone

"...he acquired a skill and accuracy [in astronomical observation] which few subsequent travellers have possessed to a like degree."

Florence Nightingale (sending a contribution to the expedition to find Livingstone)

"I send you my little mite for the Livingstone Search Fund. May God speed every effort to save one of the greatest men of our time; or if dead, to save his discoveries. If it cost £10,000 to send him a pair of boots we should send it. England too often provides great men and then leaves them to perish." (*David Livingstone*, by H. G. Adams p. 279. Hodder & Stoughton, 1884).

H. M. Stanley (writing many years after Livingstone's death)

"In the annals of exploration of the Dark Continent, we look in vain among other nationalities for a name such as Livingstone's. He stands pre-eminent above all; he unites in himself all the best qualities of other explorers...Britain...excelled herself even when she produced the strong and perseverant Scotchman, Livingstone."

Mr. E. D. Young

"His extensive travels place him at the head of modern explorers, for no one has dared to penetrate where he has been; no one has, through a lengthy series of years, devoted so much of life to searching out tribes hitherto unknown, and I believe his equal will rarely, if ever, be found in one particular and essential characteristic of the true explorer. He has the most singular faculty of ingratiating himself with the natives, withersoever he travels. A frank, open-hearted generosity, combined with a constant jocular way in treating with them, carries him through all. True, it is nothing but the most iron bravery which enables a man thus to move amongst difficulties and dangers with a smile on his face, instead of a haggard, care-worn, or even a suspicious look. Certain it is, also, that wherever he has passed, the natives are only too anxious to see other Englishmen, and in this way we must crown him king of African pioneers." (*David Livingstone*, by H. G. Adams pp. 271–272. Hodder & Stoughton, 1884.)

19

"DR. LIVINGSTONE IS DEAD!"

David Livingstone was sent out on his last African commission with two special objectives in mind. The first, which had intrigued all African explorers, was to find where the Nile, which ran into the Mediterranean Sea through Egypt, really began. The other was to try and bring the Arab slave trade to an end. He did not, in fact, achieve either objective, but he contributed a great deal to stopping the slave trade.

He sailed from England to India, and then from Bombay to Zanzibar, collecting some Indians and Africans to make up a party of between forty and fifty men, with camels, buffalos, and mules. David had heard of another great lake, bigger, they said, than Nyasa, and he wished to find if the two were joined. He made his way to the north of Lake Nyasa and then pressed northward again. The party began to grow smaller. Some deserted. He sent the Indians back to the coast. Animals were bitten by tsetse flies and died. None of this surprised the great explorer. Nor was he surprised that some of his followers were dishonest and stole his possessions. The worst of these was a man named Musa.

After David's party had been attacked by fierce Mafite warriors in the bush, Musa disappeared. Sometime later he appeared on the coast with terrible news. "Dr. Livingstone is dead!" he told the officials. "I saw him killed by a Mafite warrior. I brought some of his things away with me to prove it!" He showed some of the doctor's possessions and letters that he had stolen when he left.

Very quickly the news spread around the world: The greatest explorer of all time was dead!

(Opposite) Livingstone unlocks
the door to Africa, in a contemporary
cartoon.

37

20

IS IT TRUE?

In Central Africa, David Livingstone went on with his journey of exploration. Little news got through to him from the outside world. He was not sure whom he could trust in the expedition, except Susi and Chuma, two men who had been with him for almost ten years. Arab slave traders intercepted supplies and medicine sent to him, and stole them. Mail intended for him was, in one case, lost at sea and at other times destroyed by the Arabs, who regarded him as an enemy of their trade and of themselves. None of his own letters ever got through to England or the coast.

It was then that the Royal Geographical Society sent out a search party led by a member of David's previous expedition, E. B. Young, to prove or disprove the rumor of his death. They traced him to one of the Arab traders' crossing places on Lake Nyasa, then found a village where he had slept and where the villagers laughed at the story that he had been killed.

"Everybody would have known if that had happened!" they said.

Rumour was all the rescue party could find. There was no real news, and in December 1868 they came back to England. But by that time a letter had arrived from David Livingstone, proving that he was certainly alive long after Musa had spread the "news" that he was dead.

Even so, he certainly seemed to be lost, as far as his friends and the British government were concerned.

21
THE HEART OF AFRICA

At last a letter from David reached the vice-consul at Zanzibar in 1869. The world was able to rejoice that the great doctor was alive somewhere in the heart of Africa! But no one could imagine the difficulties and misfortunes he faced.

He was driven by the desire to find the "other great lake," and he eventually *did* discover it, and set it down on his careful, detailed map, as well as two other lakes. The "great" one was to be called Lake Tanganyika. But, on the journey, there were countless disasters. Sickness and fever were always there. A boy dropped Livingstone's measuring instruments and damaged them. Two porters deserted and took with them a box of gunpowder, two guns, all the expedition's dishes, and worst of all, their supply of medicine. Southward, "through almost trackless forests and across oozing bogs," they made their way back slowly to the town of Ujiji. Here David discovered that none of the thirty-four letters he had written had ever arrived and stores and medicines from the coast had been stolen again. He had almost no resources left, but to his astonishment, a letter from the Sultan of Zanzibar ordered the most important slave traders to give him help, and they did!

He had arrived in Ujiji after a journey on foot, in canoes, and finally carried in a litter by his faithful servants, and was almost dead. Emaciated and ill, he had no idea that another expedition had been sent out from England to find him – or that the United States also was hunting for him!

22

MR. STANLEY MEETS DOCTOR LIVINGSTONE

It was to be one of the great historic meetings.

An American newspaper, the *New York Herald*, knew it would have one of the most dramatic "scoops" of the century if it could really *find* David Livingstone, instead of merely picking up rumours about him. The editor commissioned its foreign correspondent to do just that, supplying all the money he needed for expenses. H. M. Stanley seems not to have been particularly excited about the idea, for he traveled to several other African and Asian countries before he landed at Zanzibar, picked up a rumour that "Doctor Livingstone is at Ujiji," and set off with a large party to find him.

But by this time, David was no longer at Ujiji. Recovered from his illness and semi-starvation, he set off to find "four rivers rising in one spot and flowing in different directions" and led a party of Arabs to find the place. He did not do so, but he *did* run into another danger when a party of slavers set fire to a village, dragged its men away as slaves, and David himself was pursued by angry tribesmen with poisoned spears who mistook him, as a white man, for a slaver.

Back at last in Ujiji, he arrived to find the town throbbing with news and excitement. "There is another white man here!" they told him. And as he pressed his way through the crowds of African men, women, and children, he saw a white man moving forward, his hand outstretched, and heard an American voice.

"Doctor Livingstone, I presume?" The men smiled at each other. "I am Henry Morton Stanley, from the United States."

(Opposite) The famous meeting of Livingstone and Stanley.

23
"VERY MUCH ALIVE!"

H. M. Stanley was one of the great traveler-journalists of the last century. He was able not only to send back news of Dr. Livingstone still being very much alive, but to thrill the world with his descriptions of Central Africa, of David's journeys and discoveries, and of his determination to go on until he dropped. The whole western world was excited as the news spread.

For David himself, Stanley's arrival was a tremendous thing — exciting and uplifting and refreshing. He was able to speak English for the first time in nearly four years, to hear what was happening in Europe and America, and to share his own dreams. Stanley was more interested in staying than in going home, and remained for four months. Provisions, supplies, and medicines had arrived

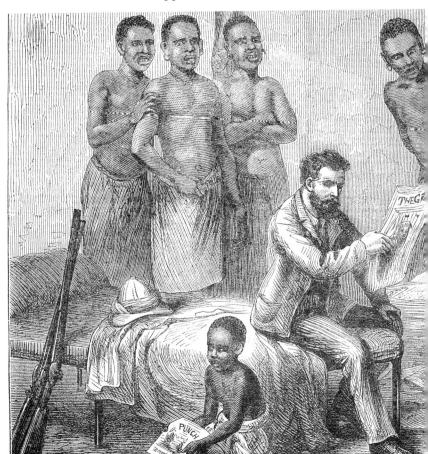

with the American; and he himself found reward enough in setting off on an exploration of the northern part of Lake Tanganyika. Stanley was so fascinated by all he shared that he became an explorer of importance when he returned to the United States.

But nothing he could say or do would persuade David to return with him to the west. "Yes, I would love to see my family. My children's letters affect me deeply. But I must finish my task. I must stay here, in Africa!" All Stanley could do was to take letters back with him which, this time, would be sure to arrive.

But Stanley left behind him plenty of fresh supplies, medicines, and a large party of men chosen by himself to support the great doctor if he chose to make any more journeys.

His next journey would be his last.

Catching up with the news from home.

OTHER HEROES OF THE TIME

Thomas Barnardo (1845–1905)
Founded homes for orphans
William Booth (1829–1912)
Founded the Salvation Army in 1865
Father Damien (1840–1889)
Belgian missionary who went to the isle of Molokai to care for lepers.
Michael Faraday (1791–1867)
Chemist and physicist who laid the foundations of the science of electro-magnetism.
Elizabeth Fry (1780–1845)
Reformer of prisons
Adoniram Judson (1788–1850)
Pioneer American missionary to the Orient.
Robert Moffatt (1795–1883)
Born at Ormiston, East Lothian, he began his working life as a gardener. He moved to Cheshire in 1813, where he came under Wesleyan influence, and in 1815 he became engaged to his employer's daughter, Mary Smith. In the following year he was accepted as a candidate by the London Missionary Society and went to South Africa. In 1819 he married Mary, and their daughter, also Mary, eventually married David Livingstone. From 1821–1830 Moffatt worked among the Bechuanas, where the natives laid out a new station for him at Kuruman. He translated the Gospel of Luke into Sechwana and continued with other translations, including hymns. In 1839 he returned to England, where he persuaded David Livingstone to go out to Africa. Moffatt returned to South Africa in 1843 and remained there until 1870.

Samuel Morse (1791–1872)
Patented the Morse Code. In 1844 first telegraph message read "What hath God wrought?"
Florence Nightingale (1820–1910)
Nurse during Crimean War; at Scutari reformed sanitary arrangements and greatly reduced death rate. Known as "the lady of the lamp."
Bishop J. C. Patteson (1827–1871)
Courageous bishop of Melanesia murdered by those whom he had gone to help.

Henry Morton Stanley (1841–1904)
Born at Denbigh in Wales, the son of John
Rowlands, by which name Stanley was
baptized. He had a rather unhappy childhood
and in 1859 sailed as a cabin boy to New
Orleans and was adopted by a cotton broker
named Stanley, whose name he took. Later
he became a writer and traveled widely,
looking for copy, some of the time for the
New York Herald. In 1869 the paper's
manager, Mr. James Gordon Bennett, sent
Stanley to find Livingstone, which he did in
1871. Later Stanley undertook further
journeys to Africa from 1874 to 1877. He
crossed Africa from east to west, which led
to the beginning of missionary work in
Uganda.
George Stephenson (1781–1848)
Built the first steam locomotive.
Nathanael Woodard (1811–1891)
Founded Christian-based, Church of England,
Woodard schools.

**(Left) Dr. Robert Moffatt and a map of
South Africa. (Right) Stanley on the
long search for Livingstone.**

24
THE LAST JOURNEY

Livingstone and Stanley parted company in March 1872. Five months later the great explorer set out on his final journey.

The next six months were the worst he had ever known. The sun was blisteringly hot, and the forests humid. The waterways were swollen with the rains, and the land itself under water. David struggled through the water, slept in wet clothes, and suffered increasingly from fever and dysentery. By January he was too weak to walk and had to be carried on the shoulders of his faithful servants, Susi and Choma, up to their necks in filthy water. Then even they gave in, and he was borne on a covered litter called a *kitanda*.

At last they reached Chitambo's familiar village, quickly built a hut to shelter him, and watched as he tossed in pain and semi-consciousness. After taking his medicine, he lay down to sleep and sent his servants to their own rest. Early in the morning they came into the hut quietly, for their master was kneeling by his bed, his Bible open in front of him. They tiptoed up to him and touched him, then looked at each other and began to weep.

The great doctor, whom they loved with all their hearts, was dead. It was May 1, 1873. Thirty-two years earlier the great missionary-explorer had come to Africa. He had spent the greater part of his life in the service of its people.

25
HIS HEART WAS IN AFRICA

His heart and his love had always been given to Africa from the moment he first arrived at the Cape. He wanted the world to know about the continent he loved, and he longed for the good things in Britain to be made available to the simple people of Africa. Most of all, he longed for the Gospel of Jesus Christ to be taken to them all. For this reason he became an explorer as well as a missionary, and more than any other man he opened up the whole of Central Africa, as he put it, "to commerce and the Gospel." He traversed it from one coast to the other. As a scientist, he made invaluable discoveries. As a Christian, he pioneered ways for the first of the new missionaries to reach the Nyasa region. He was kind, tender, and courageous, and he loved the African people with all his heart.

The one thing he detested was the Arab slave trade, based on Zanzibar, and he determined to bring it to an end.

On his very last journey he was confronted with the cruelty of the slavers time after time, and must have felt he had done nothing toward its destruction.

Yet he, above all men, helped to bring it to an end.

Within a few years of his death, the slave trade was prohibited on the mainland of Africa, both in the East and the Central territories. The Sultan of Zanzibar was persuaded to free all the slaves on the island and to close down the slave market. And, on the spot where the slaves had been sold, there rose the Anglican Cathedral of Zanzibar.

Africa probably owed more to Livingstone than to any other man of his time.

Jacob Wainwright, one of Livingstone's converts, brought his coffin back to Britain.

EVENTS OF LIVINGSTONE'S TIME

June 18, 1815	Battle of Waterloo
1825	First railway, Stockton – Darlington, opened
1826	First crossing of Atlantic under steam by Dutch ship *Curacao*
1833	First British Factory Act. Slavery abolished in British colonies
1834	Poor Law Amendment Act
1837	Queen Victoria came to the throne
1840	Penny Postage instituted
1846	Repeal of the Corn Laws
1854–56	Crimean War
1857	Indian Mutiny
1859	Darwin published *Origin of Species*
1861	Abraham Lincoln became president of the United States
	American Civil War began
1862	Bismarck became leading minister in Prussia
1865	Lincoln assassinated. Slavery abolished in the United States
1866	Austro-Prussian War over Schleswig-Holstein
1867	North German confederation founded
1869	Suez Canal formally opened